NATIONAL GEOGRAPHIC

Ladders

Common Core Readers

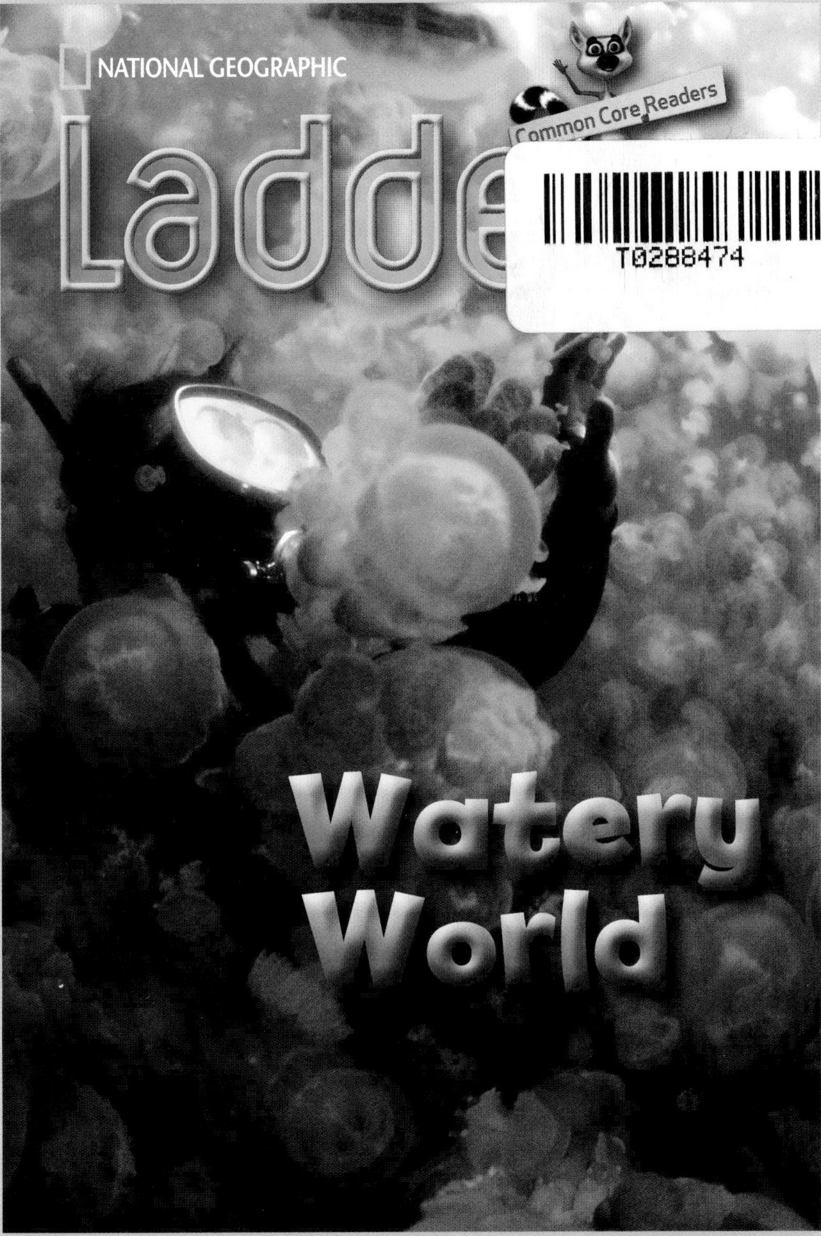

Watery World

GENRE Science Article **Read to find out** about two very different ocean creatures.

Creatures of the DEEP

by Trudie O'Brien

Every sea animal has its place in the ocean's majestic and sometimes mysterious watery world. Yet the whale and the octopus are particularly interesting. Tails, blowholes, flukes, and migration in pods make whales of any **species** fascinating to study—if you can get close enough, that is. Octopuses offer a true underwater spectacle with eight arms, suckers, ink jets, and camouflage techniques.

Species of both creatures vary in size. The blue whale is the largest animal on the planet. Octopuses range from very small to very large. One species of octopus can fit in a human hand. Another species is bigger than an adult human.

Whales and octopuses live in similar environments of the ocean, yet have many contrasts in their appearances, life spans, and behaviors. Dive beneath the surface of the ocean and get a close up look at two amazing creatures!

This humpback whale swims near the ocean's surface.

Octopuses, like this giant Pacific octopus, are mollusks. A mollusk is a soft-bodied animal without an internal skeleton.

Ocean Giants

Whales migrate seasonally from one part of the ocean to another part. They travel in a group, or pod, with a calf or with several other adult whales and calves. Scientists try to follow whales on their **marine** migrations, as this is often the best opportunity to learn about each species. How do whales know the route to their annual ocean breeding or feeding waters? What abilities do young calves have, and how do whale parents help their young offspring? These are the questions to which scientists try to find answers. How can we know how whales behave in their ocean habitat? Scientists track whales and learn about their life cycles in the wild.

Humpbacks in the same area make the same song-like sounds within a season. The songs change from season to season.

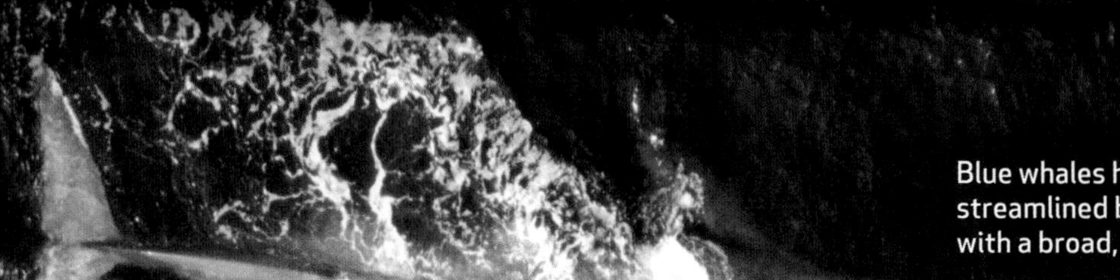

blue whale

Blue whales have a streamlined body shape with a broad, flat front part.

All whales communicate with sounds. Whales are one of the loudest animal species on the planet. Humans don't often hear the noises whales make in their underwater world. The sounds humpback whales make are song-like and musical. Their songs are communications, but scientists haven't fully unlocked their messages.

Scientists also work to make sure certain species of whale are around for a very long time. Blue whales and humpback whales are two endangered whale species. Their populations have decreased, and only time will tell if these species can increase their numbers.

Whale Size Up

blue whale

Length: 25 to 32 meters (85 to 105 feet)
Weight: up to 181 metric tons (200 tons)

humpback

Length: 14.6 to 19 meters (48 to 62.5 feet)
Weight: about 36 metric tons (40 tons)

gray whale

Length: 12.2 to 15.3 meters (40 to 50 feet)
Weight: 14.5 to 36 metric tons (30 to 40 tons)

bus

Length: about 11 meters (36 feet)
Weight: 9.75 metric tons (10.75 tons)

1 metric ton = 2,204.6 pounds
1 standard ton = 2,000 pounds

humpback whale

gray whale

Gray whales are covered with barnacles and other organisms.

The Ocean's Mammal

How can an air-breathing **mammal** spend all its life in the ocean? A whale is a mammal that breathes air through one or two blowholes on top of its head. When the whale is at the surface of the water, it draws a huge breath, closes the blowhole, and dives beneath. It holds its breath under water, swimming and feeding for about 10 or 15 minutes. When it comes up again to the surface for air, it opens its blowholes and exhales. The air it blows out can shoot water as high as 9.1 meters (30 feet). Whales may dive very deep, but they usually swim near the surface, where they can come up for air quickly.

Blue, humpback, and gray whales cannot bite or chew. They do not have teeth. They are **baleen** whales, meaning they have comb-like structures called baleen instead of teeth. The baleen is made up of plates of fingernail-like material attached to a whale's upper jaws. The baleen includes bristles, which overlap and form something like strainer or seive. To feed, a baleen whale, such as a blue or humpback whale, gulps a huge mouthful of water containing tiny animals. Then its tongue forces the water out through the baleen, which filters out thousands of miniature creatures, including krill, a shrimp-like animal. Whales then swallow the trapped animals. The bottom-feeding gray whale doesn't gulp mouthfuls of water, but it does take in both water and mud. Then it strains out the tiny shellfish that live in the mud.

A whale's body tapers to a tail with wide flukes that fan out sideways. To swim, huge powerful muscles move the flukes up and down, propelling the whale forward. The huge tail helps the whale navigate ocean waters. Whale migration journeys vary, but seasonally, gray whales swim 20,000 kilometers (12,430 miles) round-trip from their summer waters to warmer winter waters.

Scientists and curious observers alike have often observed group cooperation by whales. Humpback whales have been know to work together to round up fish for feeding and have collaborated to fend off killer sharks.

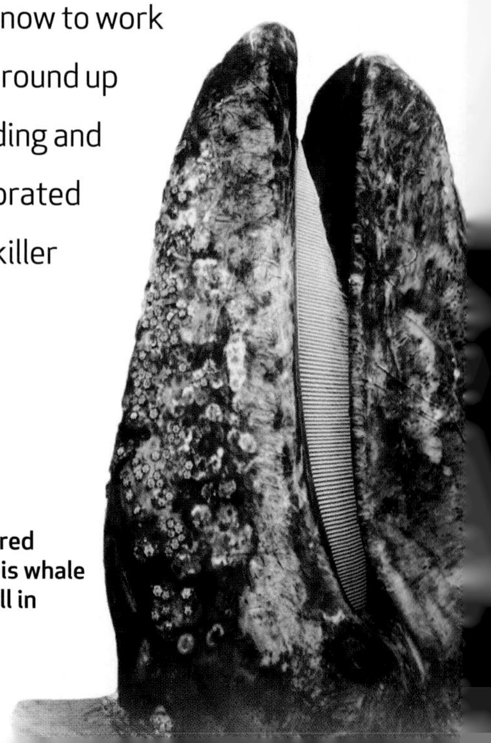

The cream colored baleen helps this whale feed on tiny krill in ocean water.

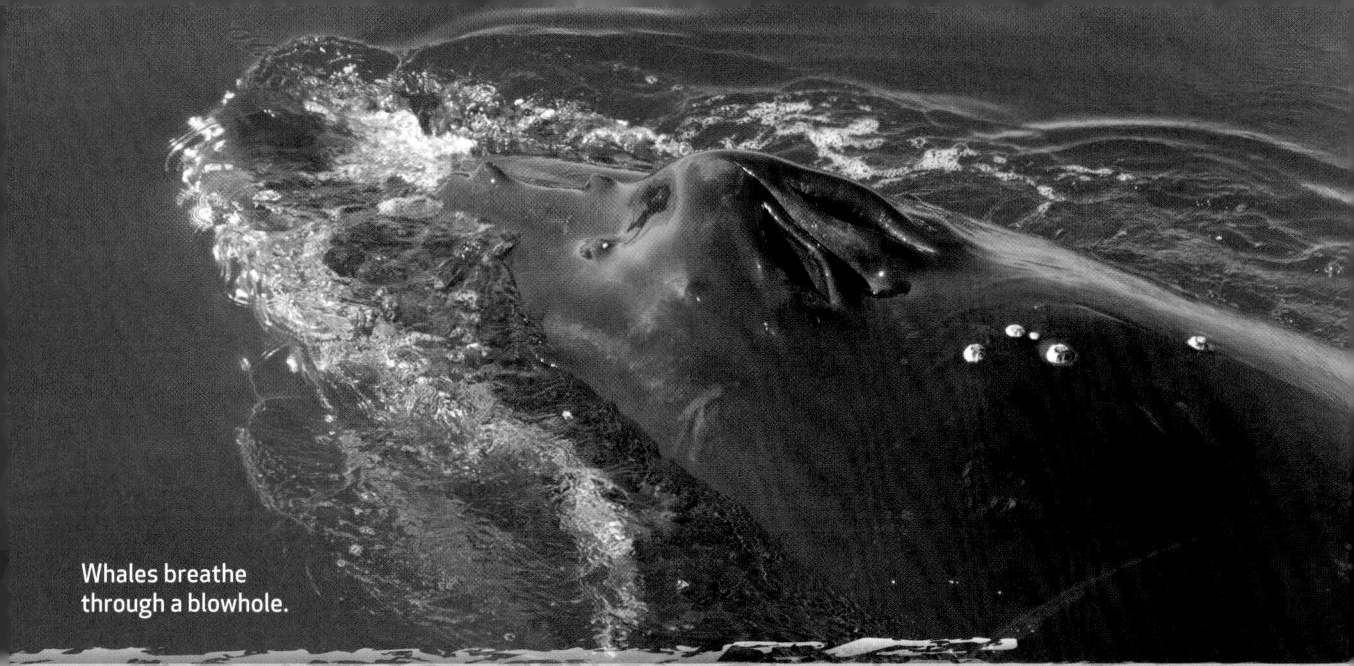

Whales breathe through a blowhole.

Unlike fish tails, whale flukes fan out sideways.

Female whales give birth to one calf at a time. Calves continue to grow and develop for about ten years.

Unusual Mollusks

Octopuses, like slugs or snails, are **mollusks** and are **invertebrates.** This means they do not have skeletons or a backbone. Octopuses have arms, sometimes mistakenly called tentacles. An octopus's arm has suckers running along it. Squid have both arms and tentacles. A tentacle has suckers at the end point, sometimes called hooks or rings.

Octopuses live between crevices in rocks and coral. Not only do their soft bodies allow them to squeeze within tight spaces, out of sight from predators and in position to make attacks, but octopuses are able to change color and texture to camouflage themselves.

Compared to whales, which may live as long as 80 years or more, these unusual creatures have a much shorter life span. Giant Pacific octopuses live for up to five years. The much smaller common octopus lives between one and two years. Male octopuses die after mating. When female octopuses lay eggs, they stop eating to watch over the eggs. Then, after the eggs hatch, the female octopuses die.

The giant Pacific octopus is the largest octopus species. It can be larger than a human. By contrast, many octopuses are small enough to fit on a spoon. The common octopus species is somewhat in between. Average sizes are about half a meter (1.6 feet).

Giant Pacific octopuses move between shallow waters to depths of 1,500 meters (4,921 feet).

Common octopuses will sometimes collect objects to create gardens or fortresses around their lairs.

Octopus Size Up

bus
Length: about 11 meters (36 feet)
Weight: 9.75 metric tons (10.75 tons)

giant Pacific octopus
Length: 3 to 5 meters (9.75 to 16 feet)
Weight: 10 to 50 kilograms (22 to 110 pounds)

common octopus
Length: 30.5 to 91.4 centimeters (12 to 36 inches)
Weight: 3 to 10 kilograms (6.6 to 22 pounds)

Many octopus species hatch and begin their life cycles as tiny larvae. They swim to the surface and start their lives as plankton.

An octopus's ink is a mixture of dark fluid and mucus. This giant Pacific octopus was swimming in waters near British Columbia, Canada.

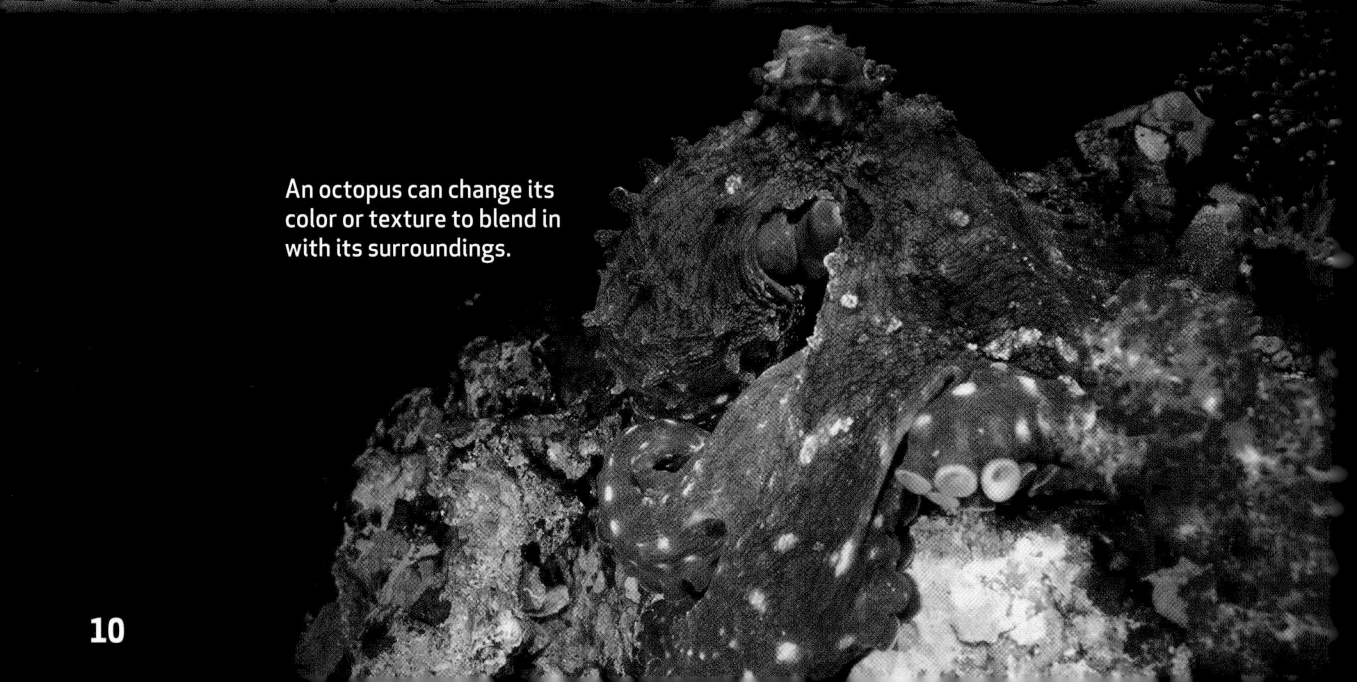

An octopus can change its color or texture to blend in with its surroundings.

Octopuses: Escape and Attack

Octopuses have heads with large eyes and beak-like mouths. Suckers on their eight arms feature sense organs, which feel, smell, and taste. Although highly unusual looking, there's a very real chance that you could snorkel right by an octopus and miss it. This master of camouflage can hide in plain sight because its skin has cells that can change color and can match the octopus to the colors and patterns around it. Special muscles in the skin can change its texture to blend in with pebbly or smooth surroundings.

If a predator does spot an octopus, the octopus shoots a blast of water from its siphon. The force of the water thrusts the octopus forward like a jet engine, and the octopus covers its escape with a spray of black ink. If escape proves difficult, the octopus can actually shed an arm to keep the predator fed and happy while the octopus jets away. Later the octopus regrows the arm.

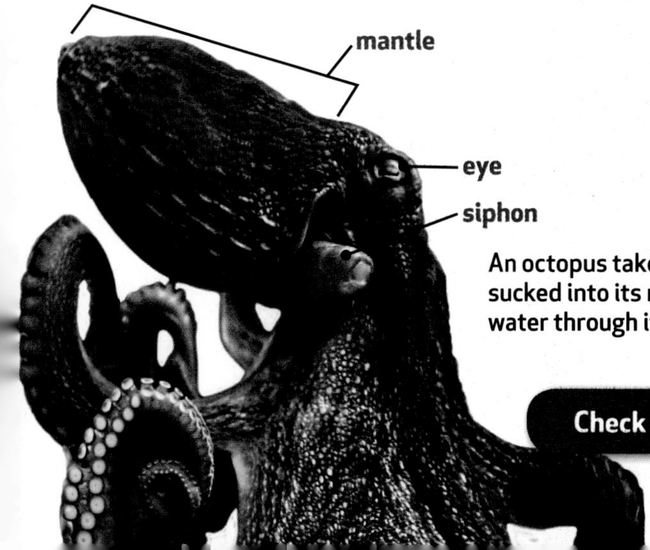

An octopus takes oxygen from water sucked into its mantle. It expels the water through its siphon.

Both the common octopus and the giant Pacific octopus dwell in temperate, or moderately warm, waters of the ocean. The giant Pacific octopus can be found in the Pacific Ocean near North America, the Aleutian Islands, and Japan.

Like whales, octopuses are very intelligent; they are the most intelligent animals without backbones. Having arms, they can demonstrate their intelligence in ways that whales cannot. For example, they can open jars, and they can solve mazes in lab tests.

Variation within each species of whale or octopus makes these ocean animals all the more interesting. Octopuses have inherited traits that allow them to quickly act and react in their watery habitat. Whales feed, migrate, breed—repeating their ocean journeys for years and years. Scientists continue to study the amazing habits and abilities of these two ocean creatures and work hard to protect their populations.

Check In What amazes you about whales and octopuses?

GENRE Fantasy

Read to find out how one octopus learns to escape ocean predators.

Sea Warrior

by Hilary Wagner
illustrated by Denis Zilber

Murdina jolted at the sight of a young blue whale barreling toward her, his cavernous mouth wide open for krill. Shivering, she dashed into the shadows of some nearby coral. Her eldest sister had told her a blue whale would never want to eat an octopus, but Murdina still worried it might just snatch her up in its gaping mouth by accident. In this whale **species,** even the calves, or babies, were enormous! Creeping out of the shadows after the whale had finally passed by, Murdina sighed wearily. Her name might mean sea warrior, but she felt more like a sea coward than a warrior.

Predator—she didn't even like the sound of the word. It frightened her, but her sister said there are predators lurking everywhere in the depths of the ocean, and an octopus must learn to take care of herself. Take care of myself, thought Murdina, shaking her head in discontent. How could she do that when she still hadn't mastered the art of camouflage and of changing shapes? She was certain she was the worst pupil in her class. Her teacher explained that her **instincts,** such as camouflage and shape shifting, would kick in when she needed them most, and her talents would develop quickly after that, but Murdina wasn't convinced. Her sister said she was a late bloomer, and her skills would manifest in time, but what if they didn't come soon enough?

Murdina thought she was hopeless because unlike other octopuses, she was unable to change color and shape, alter the texture of her skin, not to mention escape in a thick cloud of ink. Octopuses could do miraculous things, but it didn't seem she could. Kicking a tiny rock with one of her eight arms, she bowed her head dejectedly and started back for home, knowing her family could protect her. As much as she wanted to be alone with her thoughts, being alone was far too perilous for an inexperienced and awkward octopus such as she.

Abruptly, Murdina felt a cold rush of water behind her. Her heart racing, she turned to see a hammerhead shark, a fearsome predator, materialize through a cloud of silt. At first, she froze, unsure what to do. "Conceal yourself!" she whispered, eyes darting in every possible direction.

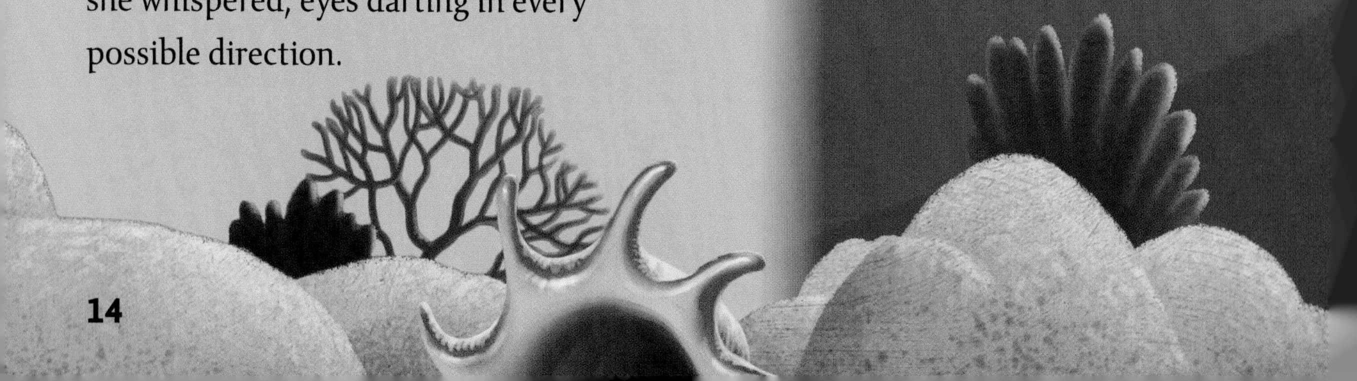

Quickly spotting the biggest rock she could find, Murdina latched onto it, wrapping her arms one by one around its smooth exterior. Nervously, she concentrated on its surface, locking her eyes on its many shades of gray. Within seconds, each brown arm drained of its tawny hue, and miniature gray and cream dots sprung up all over her body. She watched in awe as her octopus form vanished before her and what used to be her body now resembled the dull stone, a perfect match to the rock! The hammerhead sailed forward, now just over her head. It lazily glanced down at her and moved on.

"It worked!" Murdina exclaimed, watching the shark swim away. She remembered what her teacher had told her about her instincts kicking in when she needed them most. Maybe being so afraid had done the trick, forcing her to take action. Releasing the rock, Murdina headed for home, so excited to tell her sister that her camouflage finally worked.

Nearing home, the sea grew unexpectedly dark. Looking up, Murdina came to find an enormous vessel just over her head. "A ship!" she said, with a frightened gasp. Her teacher had warned the class about ships and to stay far out of their way, especially fishing ships that might be hunting octopuses.

Before Murdina knew it, her body was moving up towards the surface at a rapid pace. She looked down, realizing she'd been caught in a net, headed straight towards the fishing boat! The net had holes in it, too small for a full-grown octopus to escape, but maybe she could wriggle her way out. She tried desperately to squish her body through a hole, but with no luck. Almost unconsciously, she forced a jet of water through her funnel. Her sister had told her it would give her great speed, if ever she needed it. Instantly, Murdina's body burst through the hole in the net, freeing her. She swam as fast as she could, distancing herself as far from the ship as possible.

A surge of exhilaration flooded through Murdina. Her sister would be so proud. She did have octopus instincts after all. She spun in a circle, her eight arms rippling in the water. Steadying herself, she smiled contentedly, when a low voice came from behind her. "Why so happy, young one?" asked the slithery voice. "What sort of joyous occasion could such a pretty, succulent octopus be celebrating?"

Anxiously, Murdina turned to find herself face to face with a moray eel. It curled its slick body around her, its sharp teeth gleaming. "Don't be afraid," it said. "I don't want to hurt you." An oily grin spread across the eels pointed face. "Why I'd never do that to you, dearest girl."

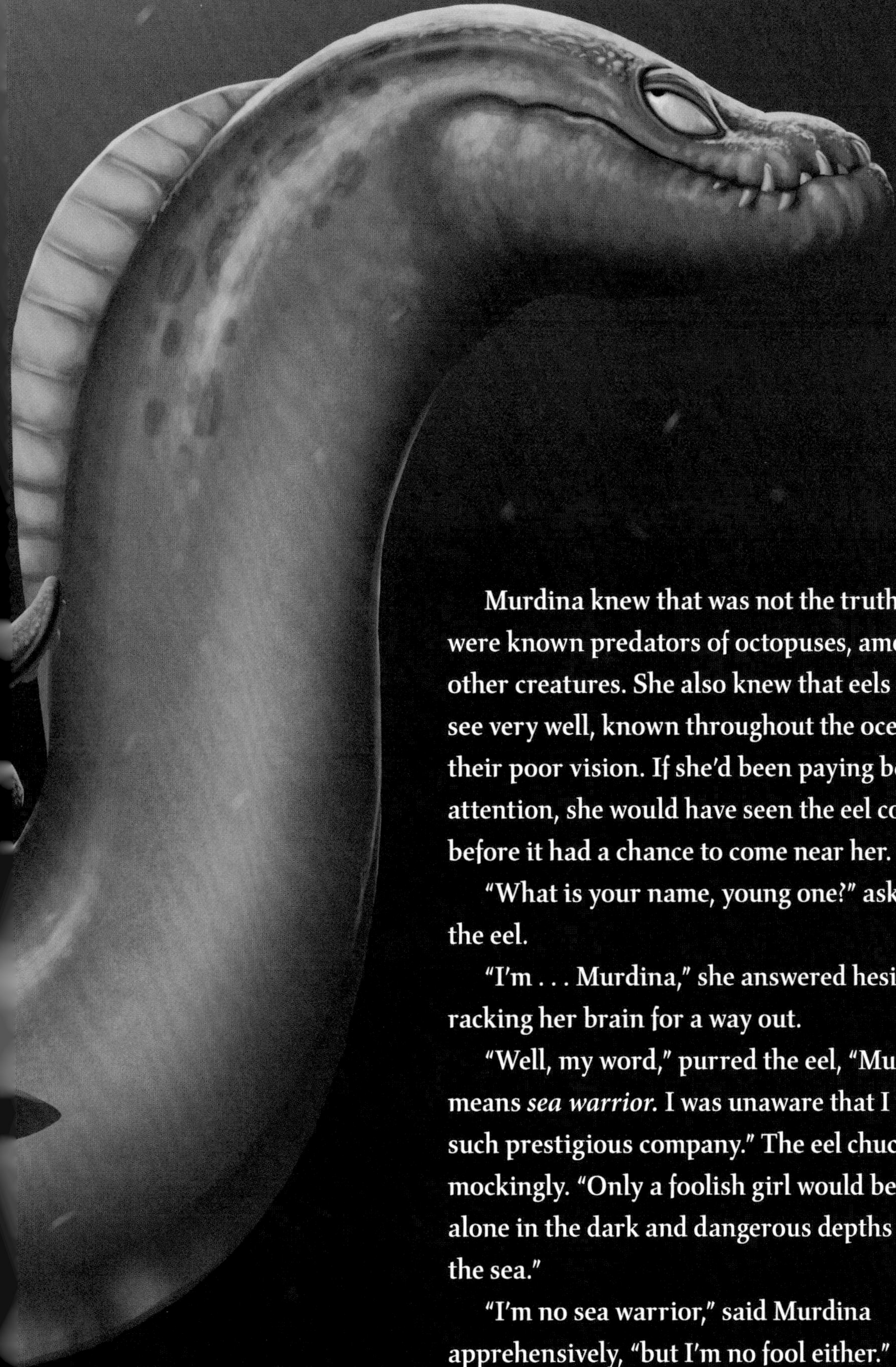

Murdina knew that was not the truth. Eels were known predators of octopuses, among other creatures. She also knew that eels couldn't see very well, known throughout the ocean for their poor vision. If she'd been paying better attention, she would have seen the eel coming before it had a chance to come near her.

"What is your name, young one?" asked the eel.

"I'm . . . Murdina," she answered hesitantly, racking her brain for a way out.

"Well, my word," purred the eel, "Murdina means *sea warrior.* I was unaware that I was in such prestigious company." The eel chuckled mockingly. "Only a foolish girl would be out alone in the dark and dangerous depths of the sea."

"I'm no sea warrior," said Murdina apprehensively, "but I'm no fool either."

Eying a sea plant, an idea struck Murdina. With all her might, she pushed a jet of ink into the eel's face. Soaring through the black cloud of ink, she sailed out of sight, quickly latching onto the base of the ruffled red kelp. In a flash, her skin changed from brown to red, the exact color of the kelp. She shrunk her body down and crimped her arms to mimic the kelp's long frilly blades, watching breathlessly as the eel swam about in a frenzied circle. "Where did you go?" it called out crossly. She held her breath as the eel glided by her, totally unaware that Murdina was veiled in the kelp.

Enraged, the eel finally gave up looking for her, grumbling to itself, as it swam away. Murdina looked all around her, now very much aware she should save her merriment until she was securely at home with her family. Her sister was right. Predators are *everywhere*. No wonder the octopuses had developed such astounding skills. Keeping up her guard the entire way, Murdina finally arrived at their **marine** burrow. Greeting Murdina, her older sister looked at her curiously. "Something's changed about you," said her sister. "Your face . . . it's so confident, as though you're a great warrior returning from battle."

"Let's go inside," said Murdina, eying their surroundings vigilantly. "I'll tell you all about it."

Check In What animal behaviors saved Murdina from ocean predators?

GENRE Fantasy

Read to find out about Charlie's favorite marine animal.

Charlie's Swim

by Hilary Wagner
illustrated by Paule Trudel Bellemare

Rubbing his eyes wearily, Charlie rolled out of bed and walked to the window of the hotel room. He looked out at the ocean, watching it dance up and down the shoreline. He'd been waiting for this day for weeks—his twelfth birthday. For his present, his older brother Seth had arranged to take him blue whale watching. Charlie had been studying them in school, and now he'd finally get to see real blue whales, not just the pictures of the **species** he'd seen in books and online. He was relieved Seth had agreed. After all, how was he supposed to become a **marine biologist** if he only saw blue whales in photographs?

The blue whale is the largest living creature on Earth, with a life span of about 80 years. With a life span that long, Charlie could only imagine how many blue whales lived in the depths of the sea. Weighing in at a whopping 200 tons, the thought of being the size of a blue whale was staggering, but then again, the sea was so vast, maybe even the blue whale felt miniscule in it. Softly, he opened the sliding glass door that led out onto the beach and crept off the patio and out onto the sand, the tiny particles sticking to his feet. The sound of the ocean gently hitting the shore was like a rhythmic lullaby. It reminded him of being a child and his mother singing to him. He wondered if young whales liked the sound, too.

As Charlie watched the frothy waves, a strident sound suddenly filled the air, blaring from the depths of the ocean. It sounded like a tuba, only lower in pitch and much, much louder. He'd know that commanding sound anywhere. It was the call of the blue whale! Charlie sprinted towards the water's edge, the waves just reaching his toes. He knew he shouldn't travel this far out to the shore on his own, but something told him he'd be fine. He took a step farther into the water, the cuffs of his pajama pants quickly soaked through. He saw something gliding through the water, the top of its rounded body just breaking the water's surface.

The massive creature in the water called out to him. "Come in the water with me, Charlie," it said, in a boy's voice not much different from his own. "Take a swim with me . . . for your birthday."

Eyes widening, Charlie made out the creature, a young blue whale. "I can't come with you," he called back, hands cupped around his mouth, "I'll drown."

"I give you my word, you'll be well protected," called the blue whale.

Before Charlie could answer, an odd sensation swept over him. He looked down at his body, now fully in the water. No longer having the body of a human being, Charlie had completely transformed into a whale.

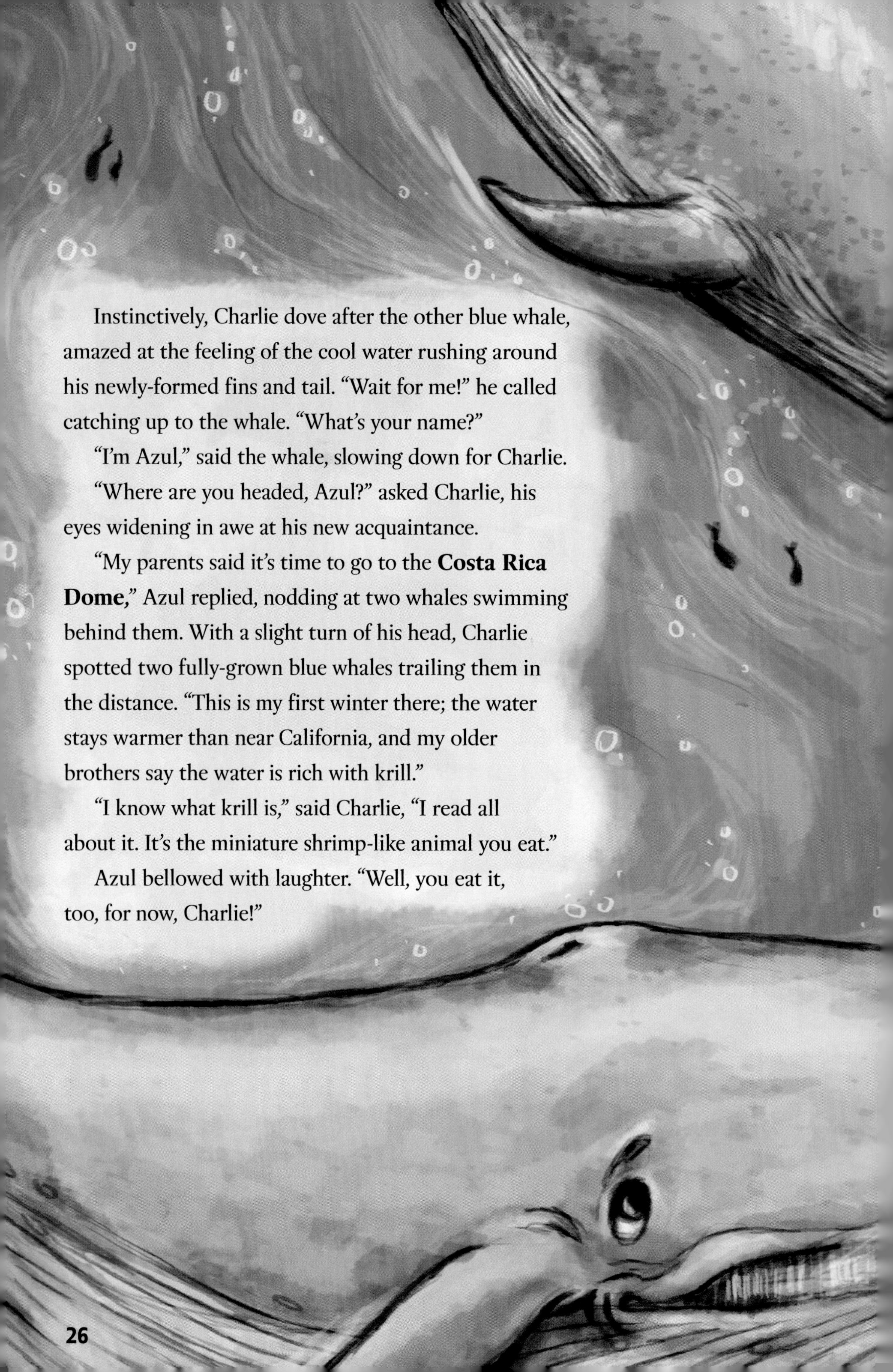

Instinctively, Charlie dove after the other blue whale, amazed at the feeling of the cool water rushing around his newly-formed fins and tail. "Wait for me!" he called catching up to the whale. "What's your name?"

"I'm Azul," said the whale, slowing down for Charlie.

"Where are you headed, Azul?" asked Charlie, his eyes widening in awe at his new acquaintance.

"My parents said it's time to go to the **Costa Rica Dome**," Azul replied, nodding at two whales swimming behind them. With a slight turn of his head, Charlie spotted two fully-grown blue whales trailing them in the distance. "This is my first winter there; the water stays warmer than near California, and my older brothers say the water is rich with krill."

"I know what krill is," said Charlie, "I read all about it. It's the miniature shrimp-like animal you eat."

Azul bellowed with laughter. "Well, you eat it, too, for now, Charlie!"

"How do you eat krill without having any teeth?" asked Charlie, thinking it must be rather problematic.

"Watch and learn," said Azul, taking a huge mouthful of water and blowing it back out again with great force. "My baleen gets rid of all the water and keeps every delicious krill. You try it now."

Following Azul's lead, Charlie filled his mouth with water and then pushed it out again, the tiny bristles in his mouth catching thousands of krill. It tasted especially briny and a little fishy, not something he was used to. He didn't really like it, deciding sandwiches tasted far better.

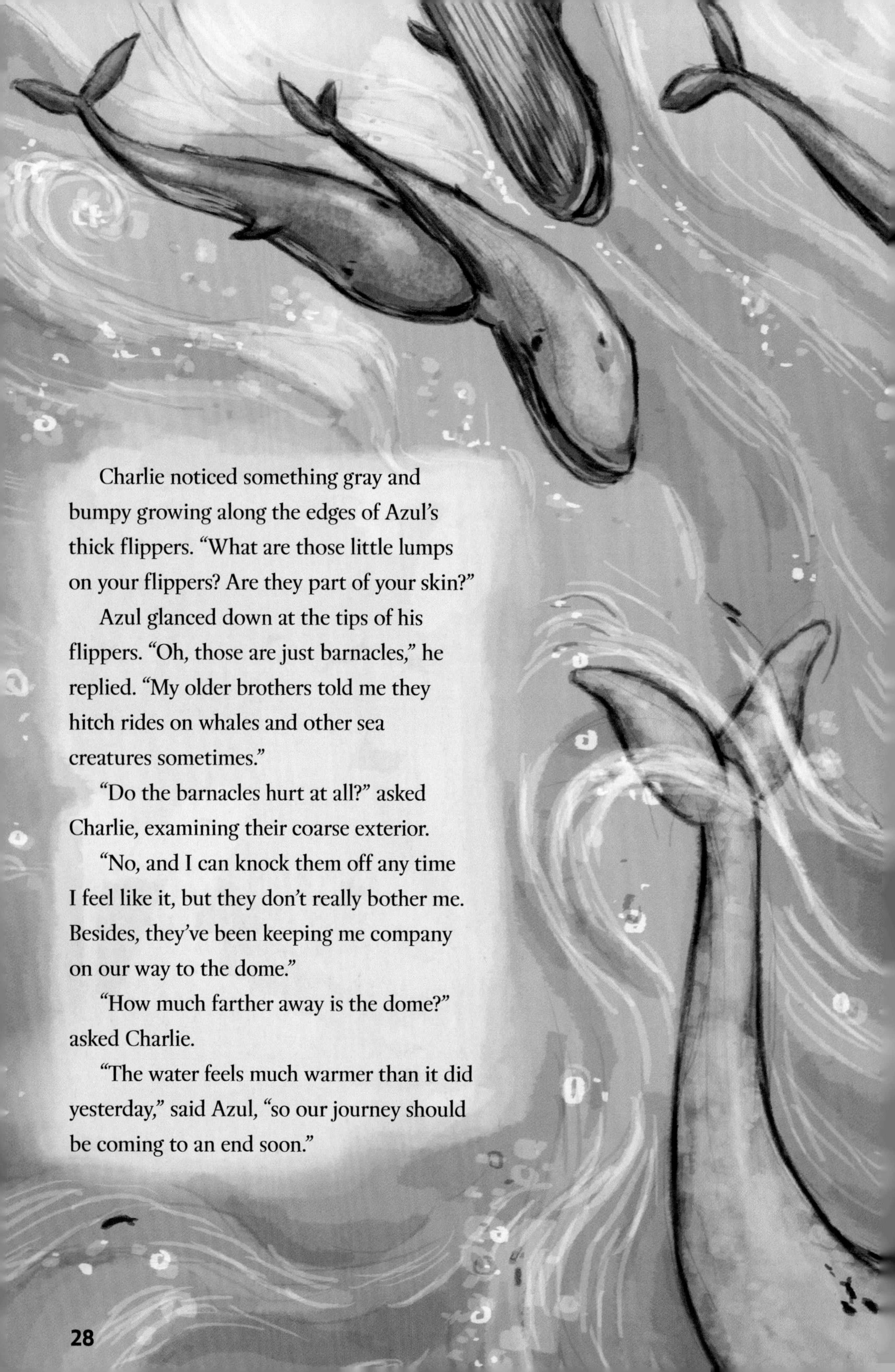

Charlie noticed something gray and bumpy growing along the edges of Azul's thick flippers. "What are those little lumps on your flippers? Are they part of your skin?"

Azul glanced down at the tips of his flippers. "Oh, those are just barnacles," he replied. "My older brothers told me they hitch rides on whales and other sea creatures sometimes."

"Do the barnacles hurt at all?" asked Charlie, examining their coarse exterior.

"No, and I can knock them off any time I feel like it, but they don't really bother me. Besides, they've been keeping me company on our way to the dome."

"How much farther away is the dome?" asked Charlie.

"The water feels much warmer than it did yesterday," said Azul, "so our journey should be coming to an end soon."

"Won't you miss your older brothers off the coast of California?" asked Charlie, thinking how much he'd miss Seth if he couldn't see him for an entire winter.

Twisting around, Azul pointed with his massive snout. Turning in the same direction, Charlie's mouth dropped open, as he gazed upon a whole pod of young blue whales, traveling behind Azul's parents. "They've all come with you?" he asked in disbelief.

"My parents said they've got a big surprise for us, so this year we all decided to travel to the Dome together," said Azul, " and traveling as a pod protects us from the orcas too—sometimes they come after the younger whales. Dad always says there is safety in numbers when it comes to predators."

It was hard to believe that the largest creature in the sea could be at risk from predators of any kind, but after today, Charlie supposed anything was possible.

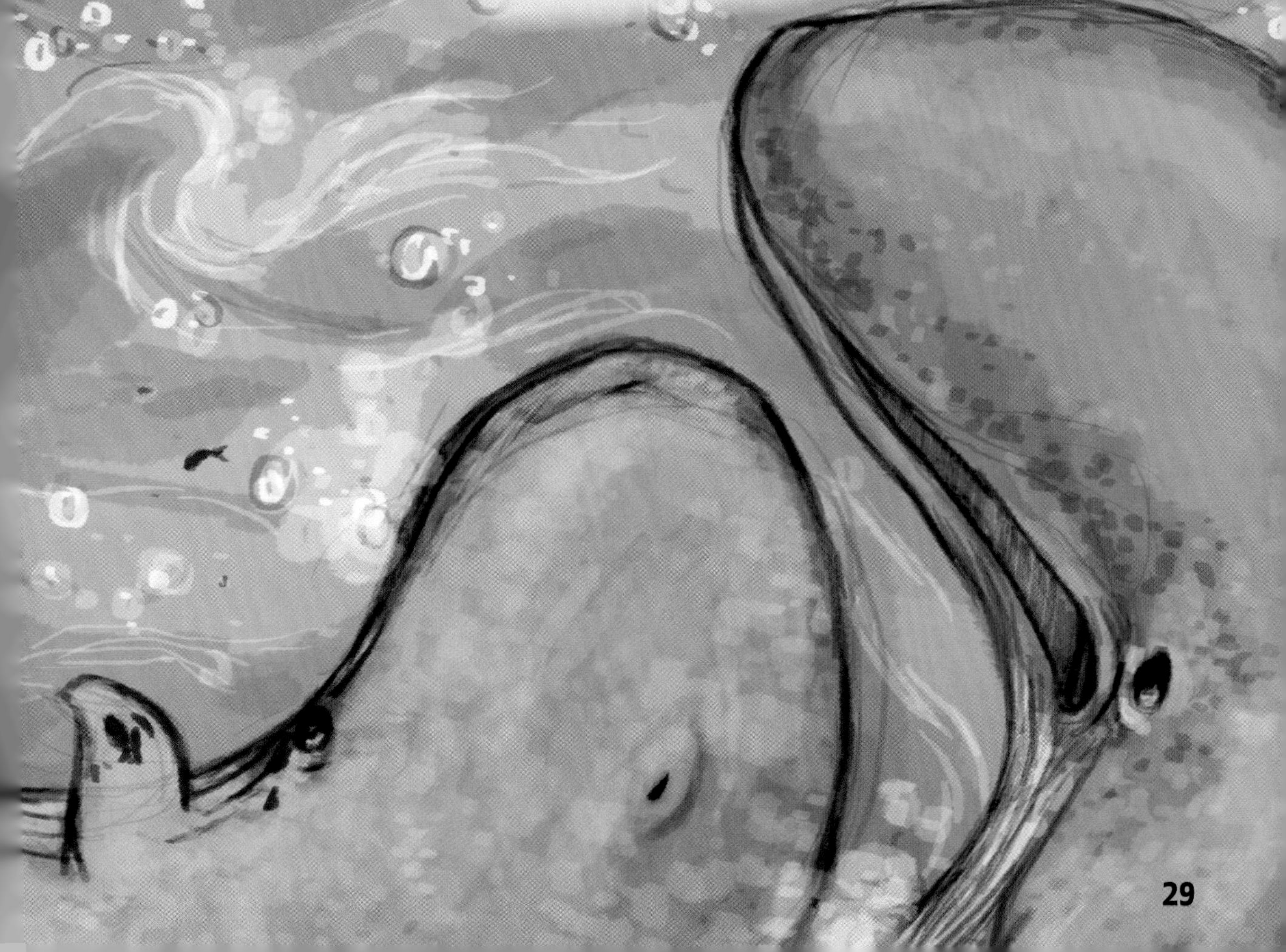

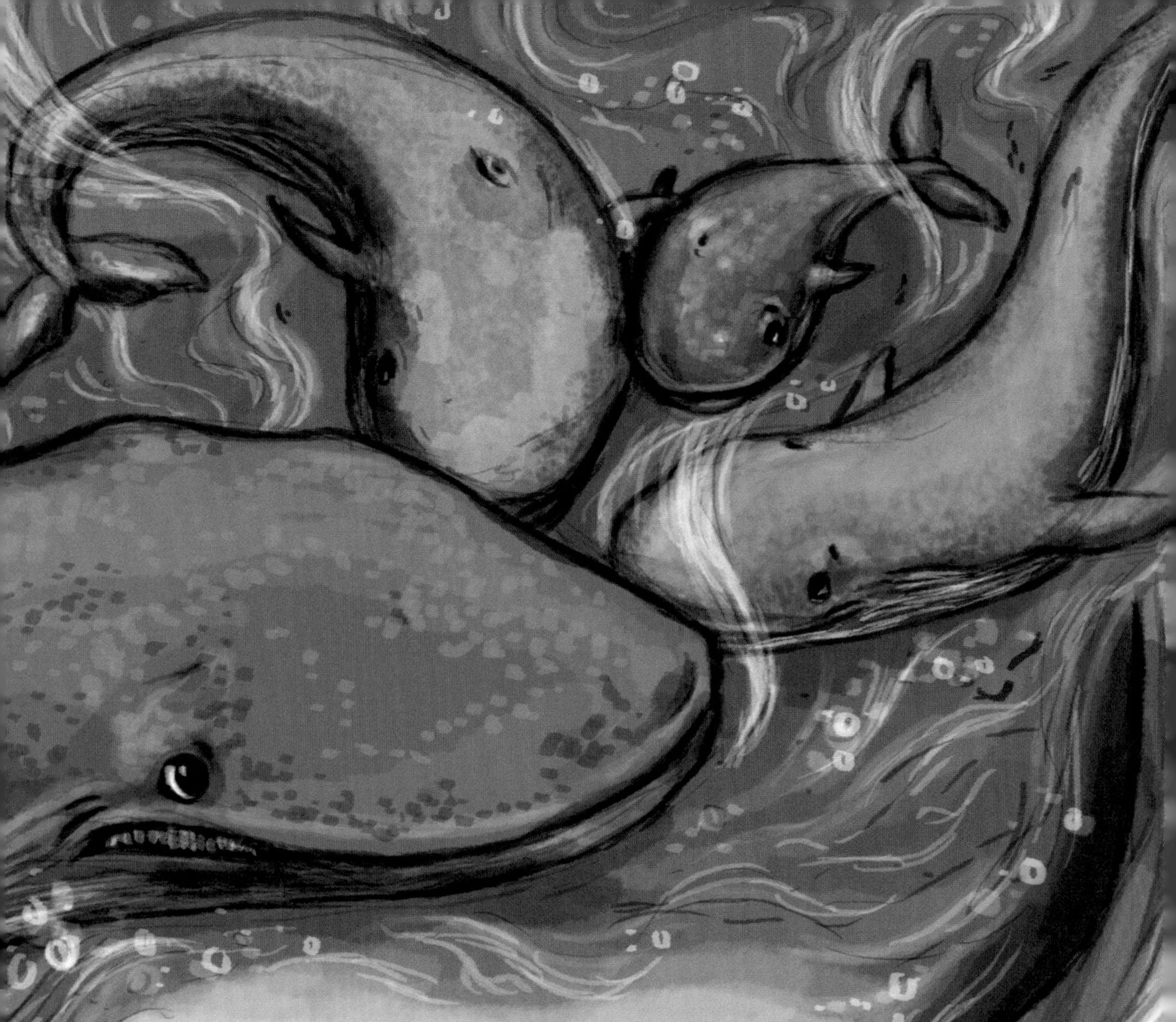

After finally reaching the dome, Azul and Charlie, both terribly hungry, went swimming for krill. Upon their return, all of Azul's brothers had gathered around their parents. "What's going on?" asked Azul, sensing excitement, as he pulled up to his eldest brother. Within moments, a small blue body soared past him, breaking the water's surface and taking a big breath of air. Azul sailed after the creature, along with the rest of his pod.

Reaching the surface, Azul came upon a small calf and gazed at her thoughtfully. "Azul," said his father in a deep voice, patting the calf with his flipper, "this is your new sister."

Azul, no longer the youngest in his family, nuzzled up against his only sister, his brothers and parents gathered around them. Missing his brother, Charlie suddenly felt very alone.

Charlie awoke to the feeling of gentle nudging against his arm. “Charlie, it’s time to wake up.” Rubbing his eyes, he sat up in bed, finally focusing on Seth, who smiled at him with bleary eyes. “Hey, little brother, it’s your birthday, time to get up and see the whales,” said Seth, taking a sip from his coffee.

Everything had seemed so authentic, thought Charlie, remembering how it felt to be a whale, swimming in the ocean depths with Azul and his family. For a moment, he was disheartened, realizing it was only a dream.

Stifling a yawn, Seth ruffled Charlie’s hair. “You sure slept late for a budding marine biologist so eager to meet the whales.”

Thinking back on the dream, Charlie smiled at his brother, remembering how much he’d missed him.

“Oh, I’m ready to see them,” Charlie said, but he thought how he already felt like he knew them pretty well.

Check In What surprise did Azul’s parents have for him?

Discuss Compare and Contrast

1. What connections can you make between the three pieces in *Watery World*? How are the pieces related?

2. Compare and contrast the two stories, "Sea Warrior" and "Charlie's Swim."

3. How are the topics of the two stories alike and different?

4. What information did you learn about the size of whales and octopuses? Compare the two animals.

5. What questions do you still have about animal life in the ocean?